English Made Easy

Learning English through Pictures

VOLUME TWO

By Jonathan Crichton and Pieter Koster

TUTTLE PUBLISHING
Tokyo • Rutland, Vermont • Singapore

Contents

FUNCTION	GRAMMAR	VOCABULARY

Preface

In an increasingly international world, being able to communicate in English is nowadays a necessity in social, professional and business life. Competence in English creates an increasing range of business, travel and leisure opportunities, opening doors to international communication.

English Made Easy is a breakthrough in English language learning – imaginatively exploiting how pictures and text can work together to create understanding and help learners learn more productively.

English Made Easy gives learners easy access to the vocabulary, grammar and functions of English as it is actually used in a comprehensive range of social situations. Self-guided students and classroom learners alike will be delighted by the way they are helped to progress easily from one unit to the next, using the combinations of pictures and text to discover for themselves how English works.

The *English Made Easy* method is based on a thorough understanding of language structure and how language is successfully learned. The authors are experienced English language teachers with strong backgrounds in language analysis and language learning. The *English Made Easy* team is confident that the books represent a significant development in English language learning.

— Professor Christopher N. Candlin

Using this book

This book is easy to use. You will learn how to speak English by looking at the pictures and words on each page. The pictures explain the words.

The table of contents tells you what you will learn in each of the twenty units. You can use this table to look up any particular points you want to learn or practice.

The twenty units are arranged in groups of five. The first four units present language and give you opportunities to practice as you learn. The first page of each unit has a list of all the words and phrases you will learn in that unit. At the end of each unit there is an interesting story which uses the language you have just learned.

The fifth unit in each group gives you the opportunity to revise the language in the first four units and to use it in different situations. The exercises are easy to understand and there is an answer key at the end of the unit.

At the end of the book there is an index which contains all the words and phrases in the book. It is not a dictionary. It refers you to the unit in which that language first appears so that you can "discover" the meaning of the word by seeing it in context.

UNIT 1: Here's a letter for you.

grandfather
grandmother
daughter-in-law
son-in-law
brother-in-law
sister-in-law
uncle
aunt
niece
nephew
cousin

arrive at
depart from
land
take off

open   on
close   off

all

lay the table
make the toast
butter the toast
pass the milk
clear the table
load the dishwasher

chair   cat
sofa

letter   postman
invitation   card
postcard   bill
envelope   stamp
parcel   fax
letterbox   airmail
email

to   from

holidays

look forward to   want
hurry up   quickly

put

1 This is the Benson family.

2 This is Jim and Peggy.

3 This is Tom and Anne.

4 They live at 2 Richmond Street.

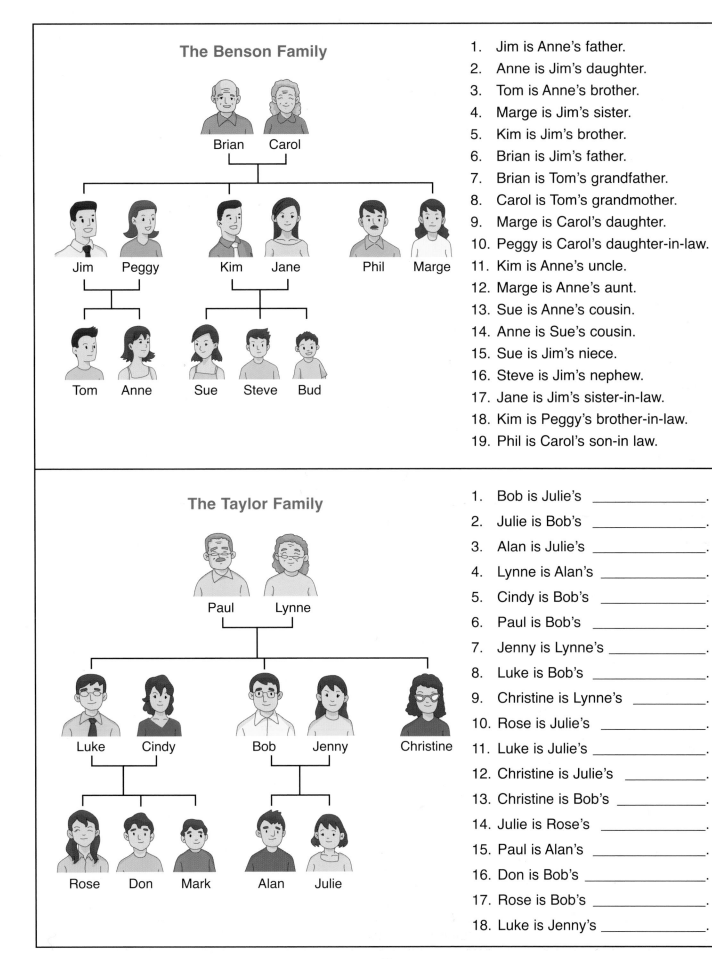

The Benson Family

1. Jim is Anne's father.
2. Anne is Jim's daughter.
3. Tom is Anne's brother.
4. Marge is Jim's sister.
5. Kim is Jim's brother.
6. Brian is Jim's father.
7. Brian is Tom's grandfather.
8. Carol is Tom's grandmother.
9. Marge is Carol's daughter.
10. Peggy is Carol's daughter-in-law.
11. Kim is Anne's uncle.
12. Marge is Anne's aunt.
13. Sue is Anne's cousin.
14. Anne is Sue's cousin.
15. Sue is Jim's niece.
16. Steve is Jim's nephew.
17. Jane is Jim's sister-in-law.
18. Kim is Peggy's brother-in-law.
19. Phil is Carol's son-in law.

The Taylor Family

1. Bob is Julie's _____.
2. Julie is Bob's _____.
3. Alan is Julie's _____.
4. Lynne is Alan's _____.
5. Cindy is Bob's _____.
6. Paul is Bob's _____.
7. Jenny is Lynne's _____.
8. Luke is Bob's _____.
9. Christine is Lynne's _____.
10. Rose is Julie's _____.
11. Luke is Julie's _____.
12. Christine is Julie's _____.
13. Christine is Bob's _____.
14. Julie is Rose's _____.
15. Paul is Alan's _____.
16. Don is Bob's _____.
17. Rose is Bob's _____.
18. Luke is Jenny's _____.

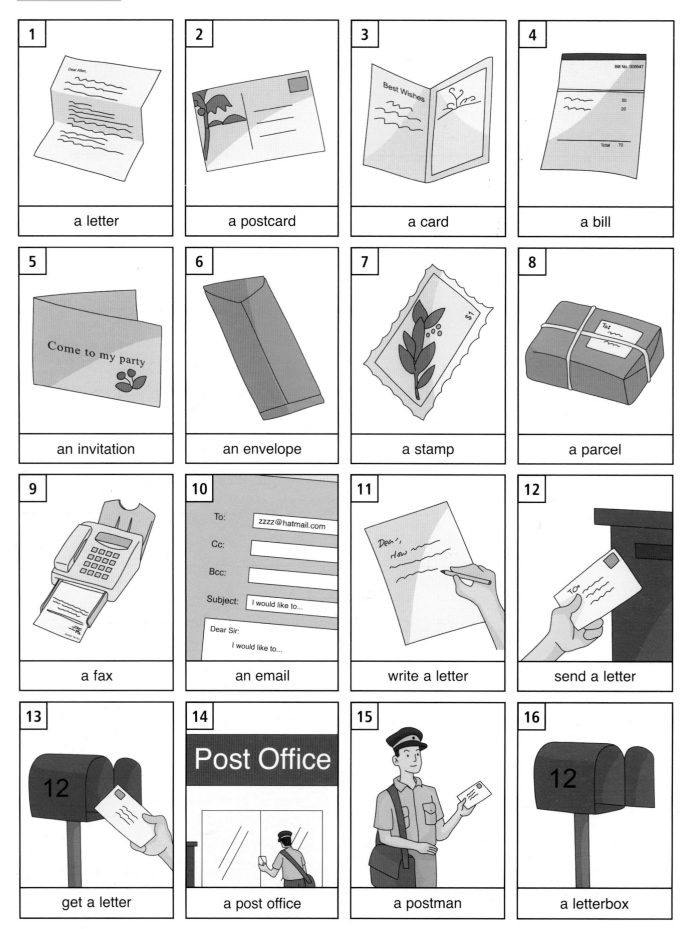

1 a letter	**2** a postcard
3 a card	**4** a bill
5 an invitation	**6** an envelope
7 a stamp	**8** a parcel
9 a fax	**10** an email
11 write a letter	**12** send a letter
13 get a letter	**14** a post office
15 a postman	**16** a letterbox

A postcard from Andy and Janet

1. arrive at the hotel

2. arrive at the hotel at two o'clock

3. depart from the hotel

4. depart from the hotel at nine o'clock

5. land at the airport

6. take off from the airport

The Bensons

UNIT 2: Let's check the flight number again.

once
twice
three times
always
sometimes
never
again

on time

right (not wrong)
wrong
check

a bit

interesting
boring
interested
bored
frightening
frightened
surprising
surprised
tiring
tired
exciting
excited

bell
ring

accident
trophy
student

say
tell

1 Say "Aaaah!"

Aaaah!

2 Tell John I'll be late.

TAXI

He'll be late.

will not = won't

21

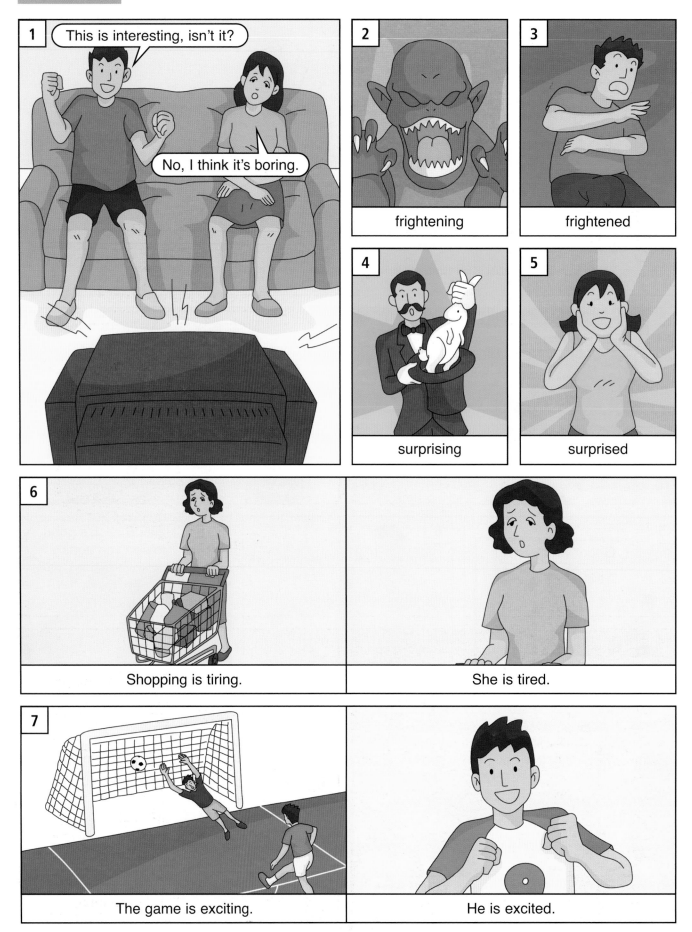

1. This is interesting, isn't it?
   No, I think it's boring.

2. frightening

3. frightened

4. surprising

5. surprised

6. Shopping is tiring.
   She is tired.

7. The game is exciting.
   He is excited.

The Bensons

25

UNIT 3: It's a goal!

half	share
equal	unequal

living room
bedroom
single bed
double bed
dining room
kitchen
bathroom
toilet
upstairs
downstairs

money

almost	not enough
enough	too much

tunnel	goal
tandem	seat

bird

lots of

front	back

tidy	mess

another

garage	shed
garden	backyard

balcony

fence
gate
path
roof

there are	there is

through	with
into	without

out of

hamburger	sauce

1

a car

2

seats

3

front seats

4

back seats

5

front door

6

back door

1. a bird

2. a roof

3. There are three birds on the roof.

4. Now there are two birds on the roof.

5. Now there is one bird on the roof.

6. Now there are no birds on the roof.

7. A bird is landing on the roof.

8. Another bird is landing on the roof.

9. Lots of birds are landing on the roof.

10. It's a goal! It's another goal! And another goal!!

1. one cake

2. two boys

3. share the cake

4. Share the cake with your sister.

5. half
   half each

6. equal

7. unequal

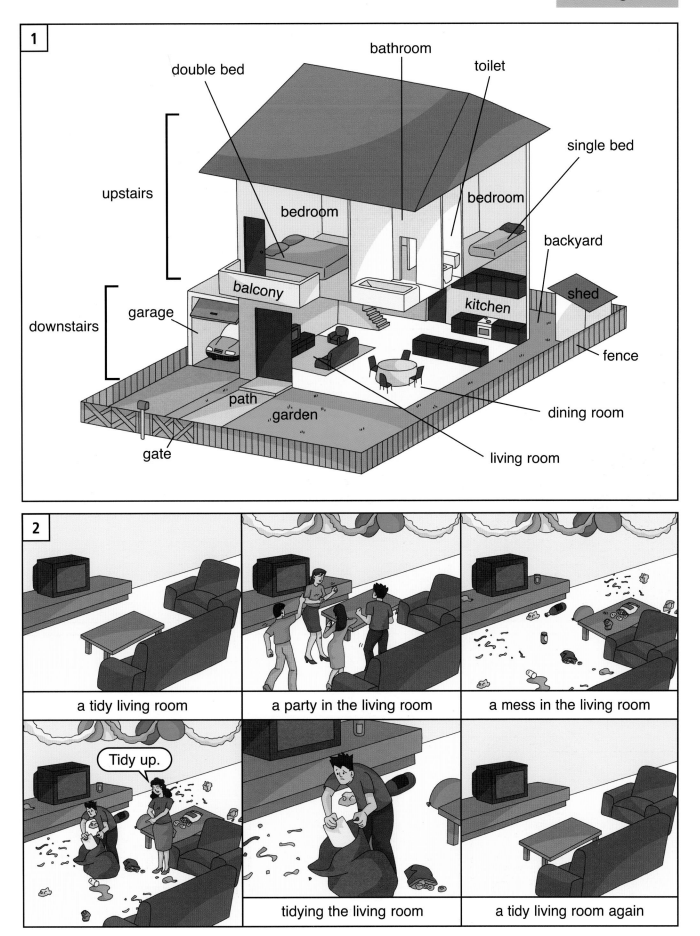

1

double bed
bathroom
toilet
single bed
upstairs
bedroom
bedroom
backyard
balcony
shed
garage
kitchen
downstairs
fence
path
garden
dining room
gate
living room

2

a tidy living room

a party in the living room

a mess in the living room

Tidy up.

tidying the living room

a tidy living room again

29

1

money

This watch costs $50.00.

This is enough money.

Not enough money.

Almost enough money.

Too much money.

Here's your change.

Not enough change.

2

a tunnel

There's a train going into the tunnel.

There's a train going through the tunnel.

There's a train coming out of the tunnel.

1 a hamburger

2 a hamburger with sauce

3 tea

4 tea without milk

5 a tandem

6 with his friend

7 without his friend

The Bensons

33

birthday
anniversary

excellent

around
around here

walk

while

chocolate bar

stars
world
trip
zoo

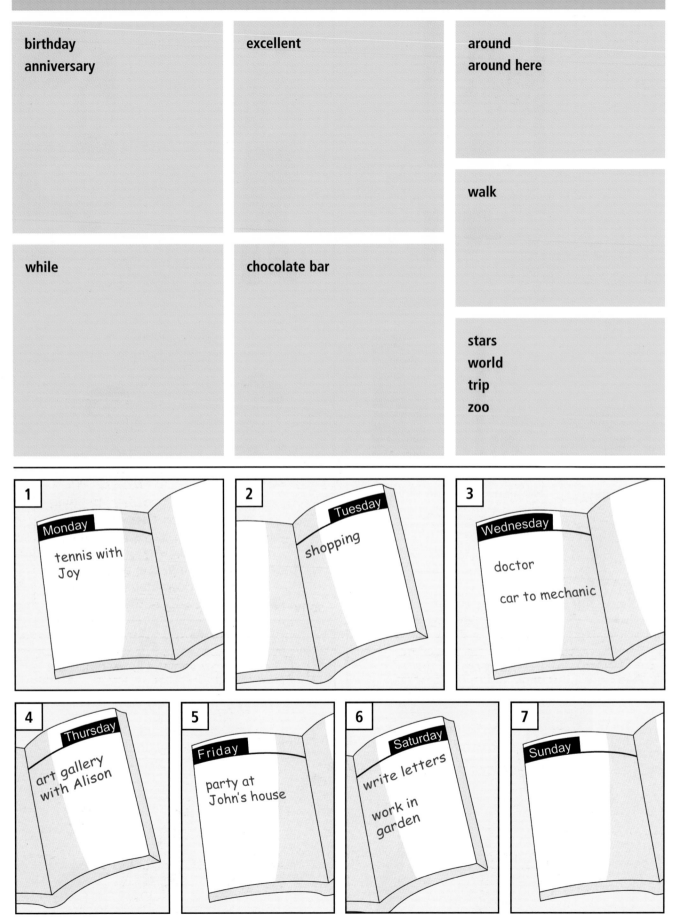

1 Monday — tennis with Joy

2 Tuesday — shopping

3 Wednesday — doctor / car to mechanic

4 Thursday — art gallery with Alison

5 Friday — party at John's house

6 Saturday — write letters / work in garden

7 Sunday

1 I'm very busy this week. On Monday I'm playing tennis with Joy. On Tuesday I'm going shopping. On Wednesday I'm seeing the doctor and taking the car to the mechanic. On Thursday I'm going to the art gallery with Alison. On Friday I'm going to a party at John's house. And on Saturday I'm writing some letters and working in the garden.

2 What are you doing on Sunday?

3 I don't know. I think I'll sleep all day!

1

28 September 1982

2

It's his first birthday.
He's one year old today.

3

It's his second birthday.
He's two years old today.

4

I'm ten!

It's his birthday.
He's ten years old today.

5

I'm 21 today.

It's his birthday. He's 21 today.

6

Is it my birthday today?

Yes, it is. You're 90 today.

7

4th August 2000

It's their first anniversary.

It's their fiftieth anniversary.

1. around the book

2. There's a fence around this house.

3. around the world

4. I'm going for a trip around the world.

5. a city block

6. walk

7. walk around the block

8. Where's my book?
   Here.

9. Where's my book?
   It's around here somewhere.

10. Where are my glasses?
    I don't know. They're around here somewhere.

11. Do you like this restaurant?
    Yes, I think it's the best restaurant around here.

The Bensons

42

UNIT 5: Revision and extension

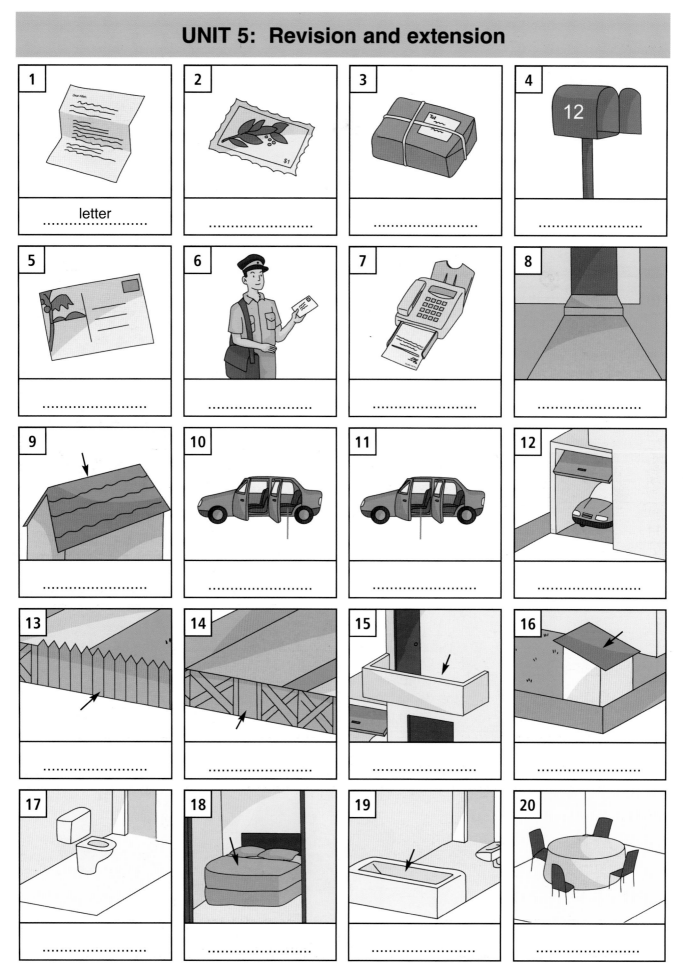

1 letter

2

3

4

5

6

7

8

9

10

11

12

13

14

15

16

17

18

19

20

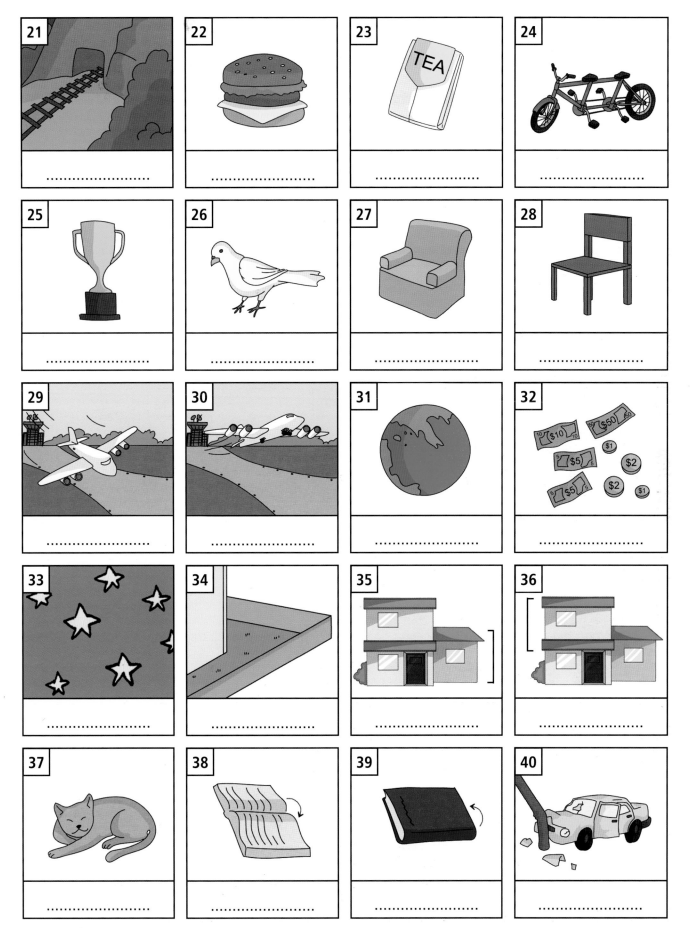

A

1. How was the flight?

2. Good to see you again.

3. I'll meet you at the airport.

4. Have you been to the art gallery?

5. This is my new car.

a. It looks great.

b. Thanks.

c. It's been a long time.

d. It was OK.

e. No, I haven't.

B

1. How have you been?

2. Where did you go last weekend?

3. Where are they going tomorrow night?

4. What are you doing tomorrow?

5. How can I help?

a. Very good.

b. I stayed at home.

c. Load the dishwasher.

d. I'm working.

e. They're going to a restaurant.

C

1. A parcel's arrived for you.

2. I'm looking forward to the flight.

3. When did the fax arrive?

4. Can we go to the movie tonight?

a. Yesterday morning.

b. Good idea.

c. Who's it from?

d. So am I.

D

1. I want to go to a restaurant.

2. This is delicious.

3. What's the best hotel around here?

4. Is this restaurant good?

a. No, and it's expensive.

b. The Grand Hotel.

c. I'd rather see a movie.

d. Thank you.

message   idea   know   How   say   another   late   happened

What   are   about   to   sounds   been   another   And   time

time   before   around   bit   looking   but   at   meet   go

them   from   sent   wrong   a   won't   says   flight

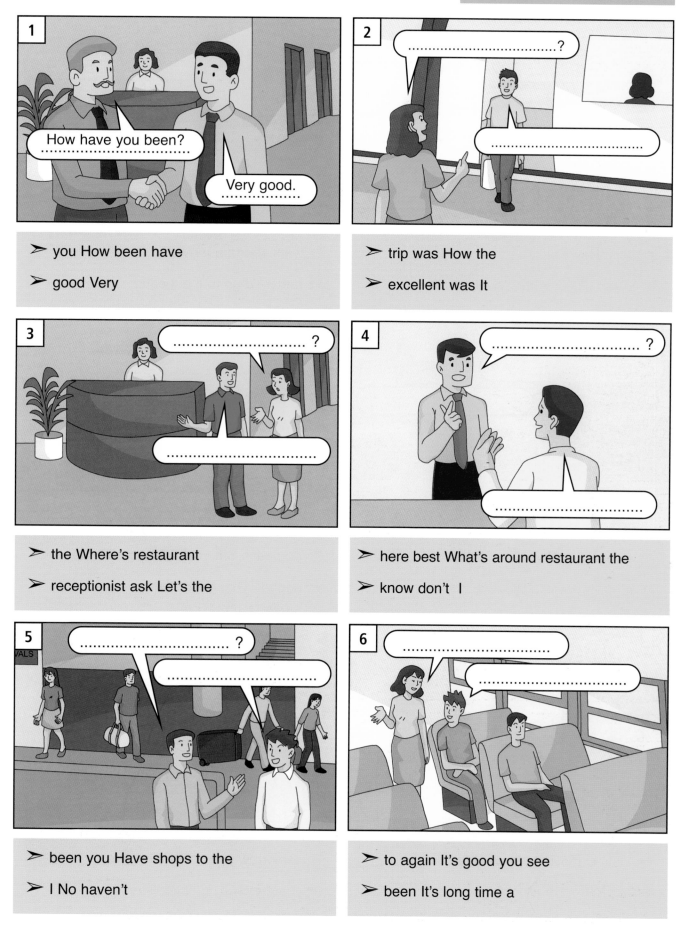

1

How have you been?

Very good.

➤ you How been have

➤ good Very

2

.....................................?

....

➤ trip was How the

➤ excellent was It

3

.... ?

....

➤ the Where's restaurant

➤ receptionist ask Let's the

4

.... ?

....

➤ here best What's around restaurant the

➤ know don't I

5

.... ?

....

➤ been you Have shops to the

➤ I No haven't

6

....

....

➤ to again It's good you see

➤ been It's long time a

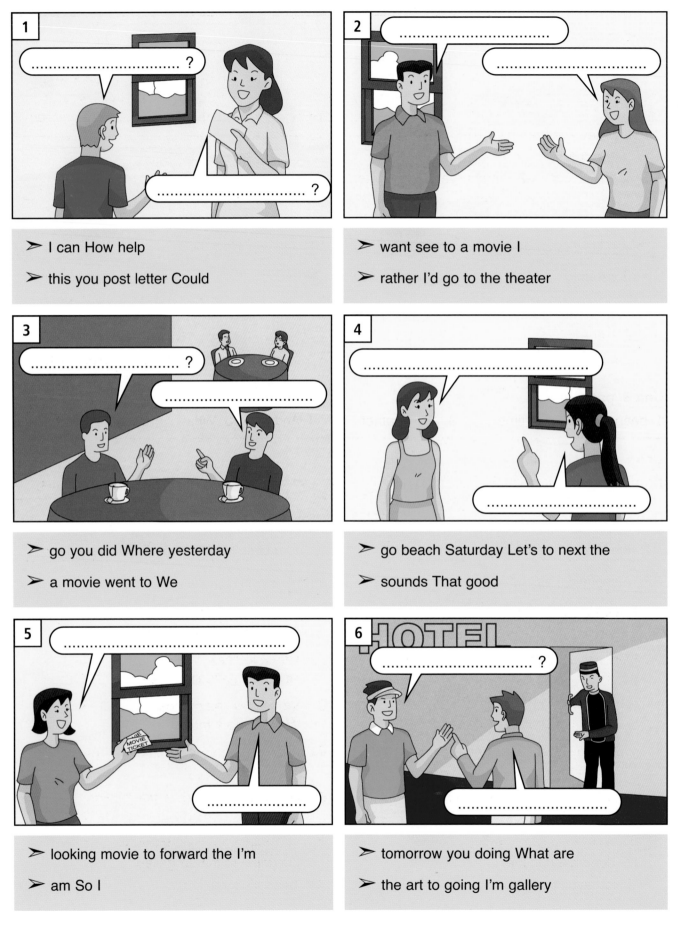

1
➤ I can How help
➤ this you post letter Could

2
➤ want see to a movie I
➤ rather I'd go to the theater

3
➤ go you did Where yesterday
➤ a movie went to We

4
➤ go beach Saturday Let's to next the
➤ sounds That good

5
➤ looking movie to forward the I'm
➤ am So I

6
➤ tomorrow you doing What are
➤ the art to going I'm gallery

Answers to Unit 5

Unit 5, page 44

1. letter	2. stamp	3. parcel	4. letterbox	5. postcard
6. postman	7. fax	8. path	9. roof	10. back seat
11. front seat	12. garage	13. fence	14. gate	15. balcony
16. shed	17. toilet	18. double bed	19. bath	20. dining room

Unit 5, page 45

21. tunnel	22. hamburger	23. tea	24. tandem	25. trophy
26. bird	27. sofa	28. chair	29. land	30. take off
31. world	32. money	33. stars	34. backyard	35. upstairs
36. downstairs	37. cat	38. open	39. closed	40. accident

Unit 5, page 46

A. 1d 2c 3b 4e 5a   B. 1a 2b 3e 4d 5c   C. 1c 2d 3a 4b   D. 1c 2d 3b 4a

Unit 5, page 47

1. happened   2. know, say   3. another   4. idea   5. How   6. message, late

Unit 5, page 48

1. been, to   2. time   3. are, another   4. And   5. What   6. about, sounds

Unit 5, page 49

1. go   2. but, time   3. at, before   4. around, bit   5. meet   6. looking

Unit 5, page 50

1. from   2. flight, them   3. says, wrong   4. sent   5. won't   6. a

Unit 5, page 51

1. How have you been?
   Very good.

2. How was the trip?
   It was excellent.

3. Where's the restaurant?
   Let's ask the receptionist.

4. What's the best restaurant around here?
   I don't know.

5. Have you been to the shops?
   No I haven't.

6. It's good to see you again.
   It's been a long time.

Unit 5, page 52

1. How can I help?
   Could you post this letter?

2. I want to see a movie.
   I'd rather go to the theater.

3. Where did you go yesterday?
   We went to a movie.

4. Let's go to the beach next Saturday.
   That sounds good.

5. I'm looking forward to the movie.
   So am I.

6. What are you doing tomorrow?
   I'm going to the art gallery.

UNIT 6: You always watch movies!

switch
turn on
turn off

radio
kettle
light
computer
printer

loud
soft
turn up
turn down
remote control
channel
fish

I'd rather
instead

fine	sunny
cloudy	showers
wet	rain
windy	snow
storm	foggy

thermometer
temperature
hot   cold

weather report
weather forecast

plane crash
news
advertisement
sport
comedy

alone
together
visit

do the dishes

hope
disappointed

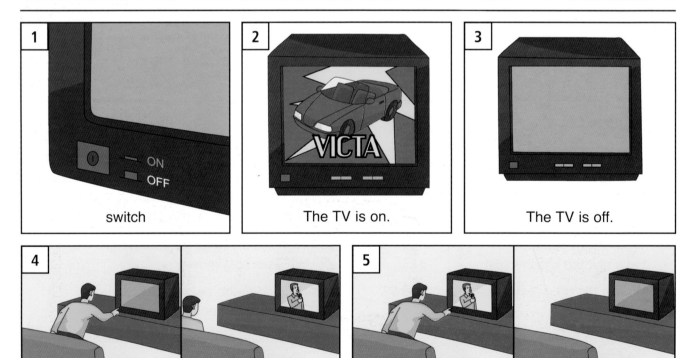

1 switch

2 The TV is on.

3 The TV is off.

4 turn the TV on

5 turn the TV off

1 a radio	**2** an electric kettle	**3** a light	**4** a computer	**5** a printer

6

loud

Turn it down.

Turn it up.

Turn it off.

7 remote control	**8** channel 3	**9** channel 6

weather

1. a fine day, a sunny day
2. a cloudy day
3. a windy day
4. a rainy day, a wet day
5. showers
6. snow
7. a storm
8. fog

temperature

9. a thermometer
10. 80 degrees — hot
11. 3 degrees — cold
12. It was hot today with the temperature at thirty degrees.

TODAY 30°
TOMORROW 23°

a weather report

13. Tomorrow will be fine and sunny. The temperature will be 23 degrees.

TODAY
TOMORROW 23°

a weather forecast

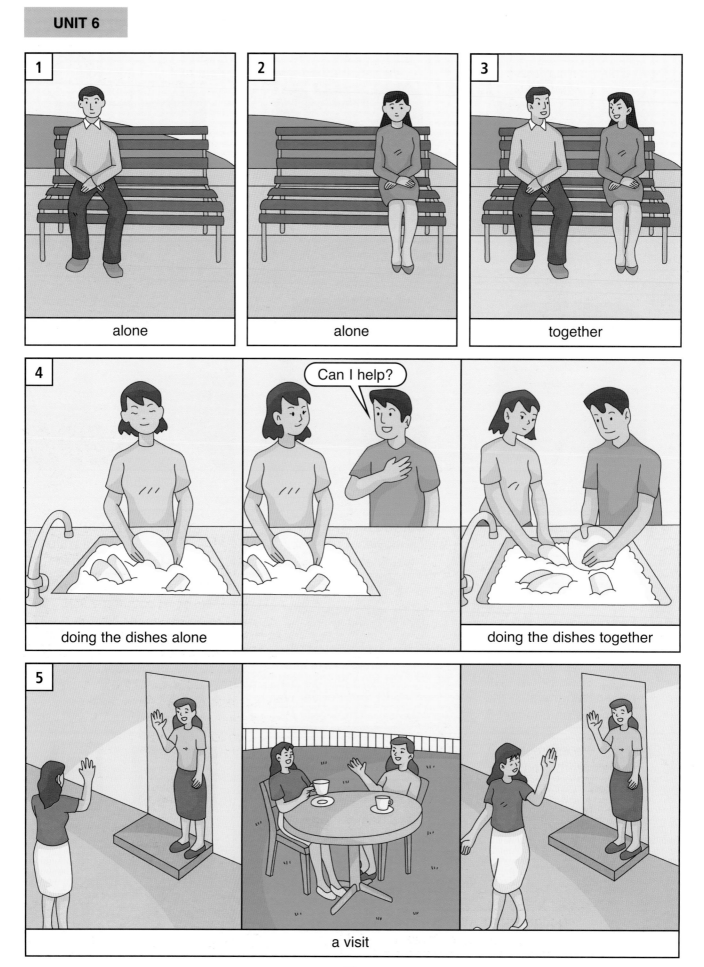

1. alone

2. alone

3. together

4. doing the dishes alone

Can I help?

doing the dishes together

5. a visit

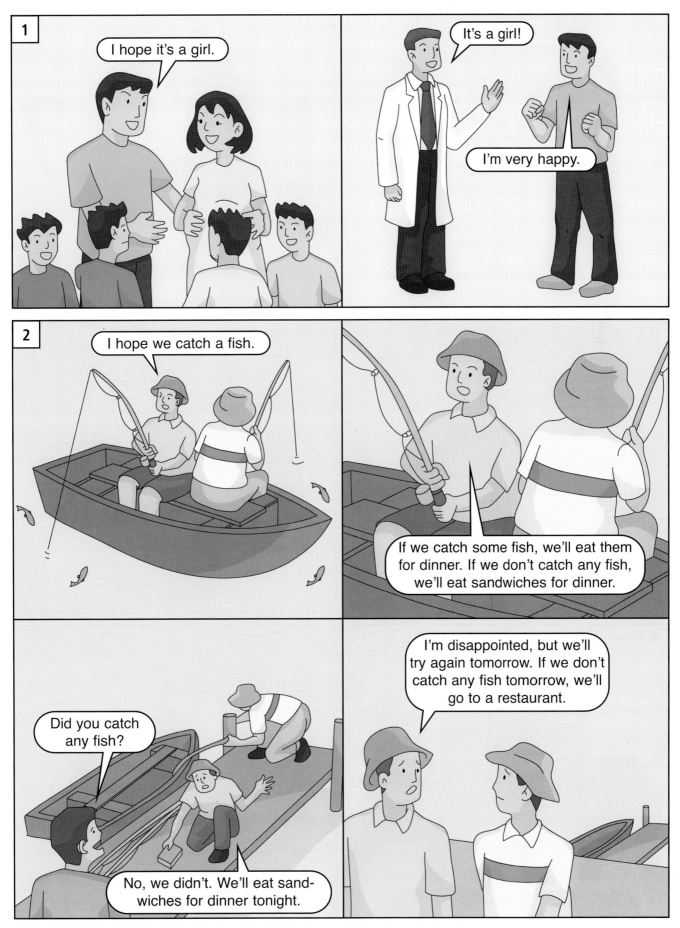

The Bensons

comb	express	ticket office
lipstick	via	platform
mascara		kiosk
eyelash		newsagent
face	twin	waiting room
powder	umbrella	luggage
hair		attendant
		timetable
busy	which	entry
		exit
ready	because	toilets
	so	lost property
go away		
come back		
return	pick up	forget
single		remember

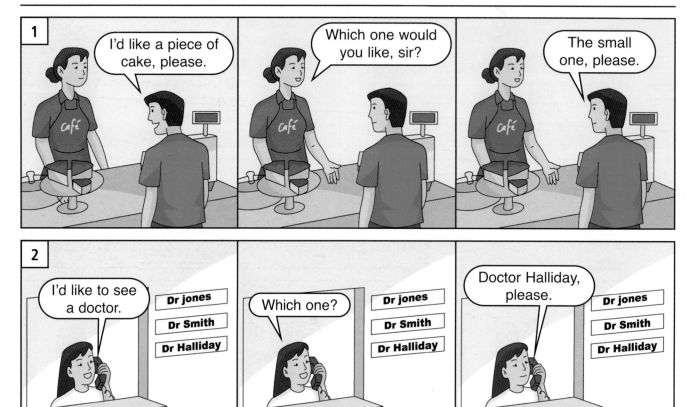

1. hair
2. comb
3. lips
4. lipstick
5. eyelashes
6. mascara
7. face
8. powder

65

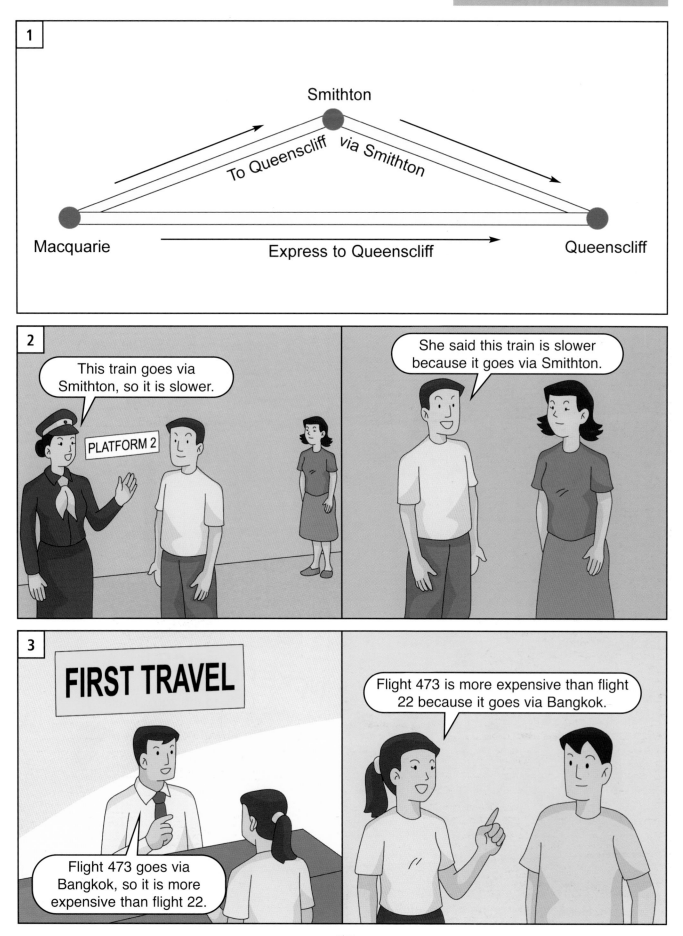

The Bensons

UNIT 8: Ten dollars extra.

who
where
when
how
why
what

start
finish
take

tour

extra

separate
join

operation

tree
trunk
branch
leaf

hill

ice
lion
tiger
giraffe
antelope
koala
kangaroo
seal
elephant
zebra
fur
pouch

top
bottom

1 finish

5 **4** **3** **2** **1**

start

2

Meeting:
1 p.m.- 2 p.m.

The meeting starts at one o'clock and finishes at two o'clock.

The meeting takes an hour.

3

DEPART TOKYO
11 A.M.

ARRIVE SYDNEY
7 P.M.

DEPART TOKYO
11 A.M.

ARRIVE SYDNEY
7 P.M.

The flight _____ at eleven o'clock and _____ at seven o'clock.

The flight takes eight hours.

Ten dollars extra.

Elephants

Giraffes

Zebras

Tigers

Lions

Antelopes

Kangaroos

Seals

Ice

Koalas

The Bensons

vending machine
hotel lobby

room service

not … enough

on
beside
behind
around
over
under
in front of

open
closed

horse
jockey
race

maybe
might
possibly
probably

boxer
fight

walk
stand
run
crawl
fly
lie
sit

wardrobe

close
far
further

1  a chair	**2** 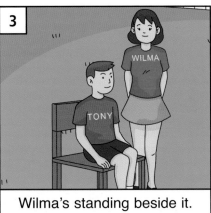 Tony's sitting on it.	**3** Wilma's standing beside it.
4 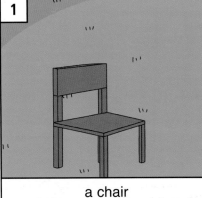 Bob's walking behind it.	**5**  Paul's running around it.	**6**  A bird's flying over it.

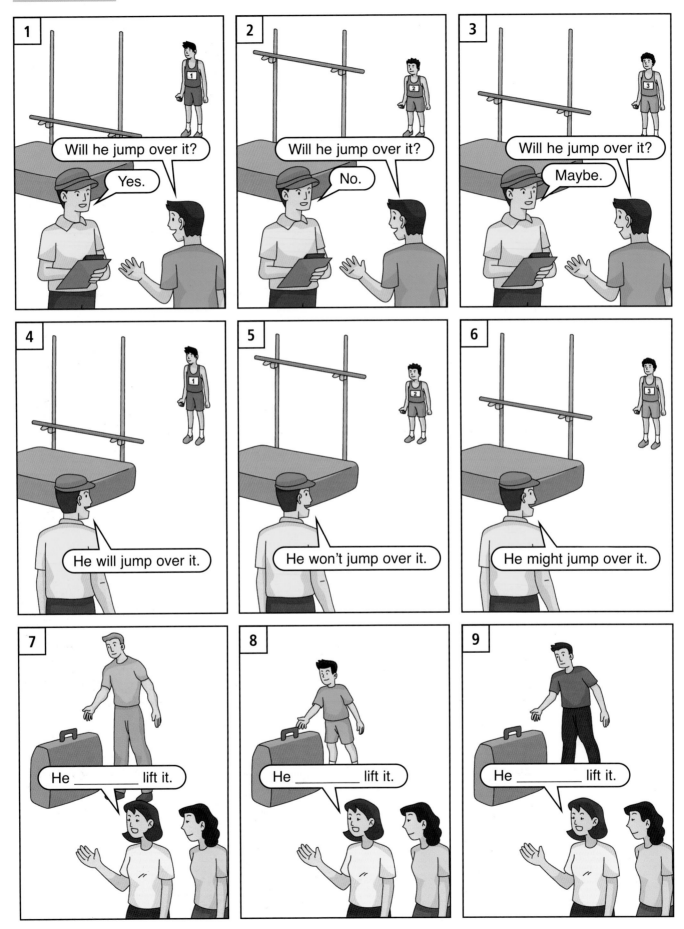

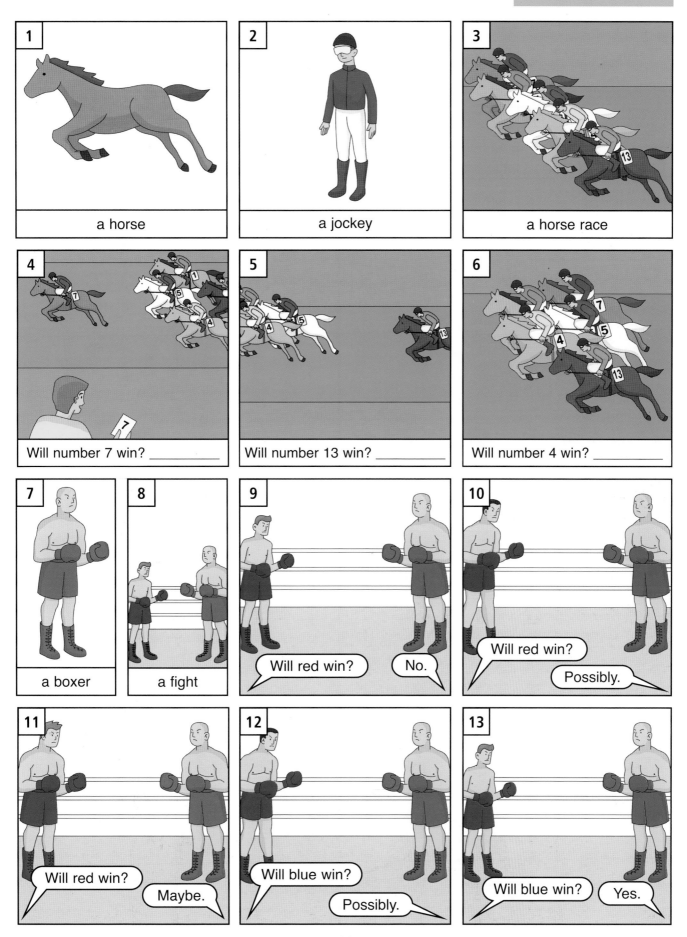

81

1 a vending machine

2 a hotel lobby

3 room service

4 reception

5
I'd like something to eat.

Maybe the restaurant is still open. I'll ask at reception.

6
Is the restaurant still open?

I'm sorry sir, the restaurant is closed now.

7
You can get a room service and there's a vending machine in the hotel lobby.

Thank you.

8
Let's go out. There's probably a restaurant open around here somewhere.

Yes, good idea.

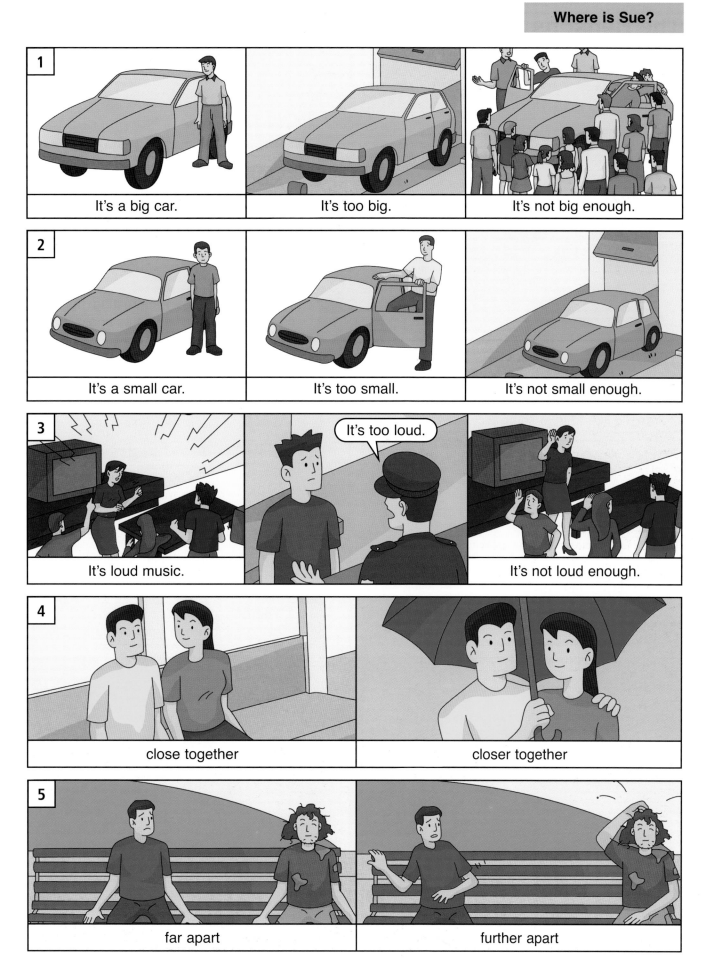

1
It's a big car.
It's too big.
It's not big enough.

2
It's a small car.
It's too small.
It's not small enough.

3
It's loud music.
It's too loud.
It's not loud enough.

4
close together
closer together

5
far apart
further apart

The Bensons

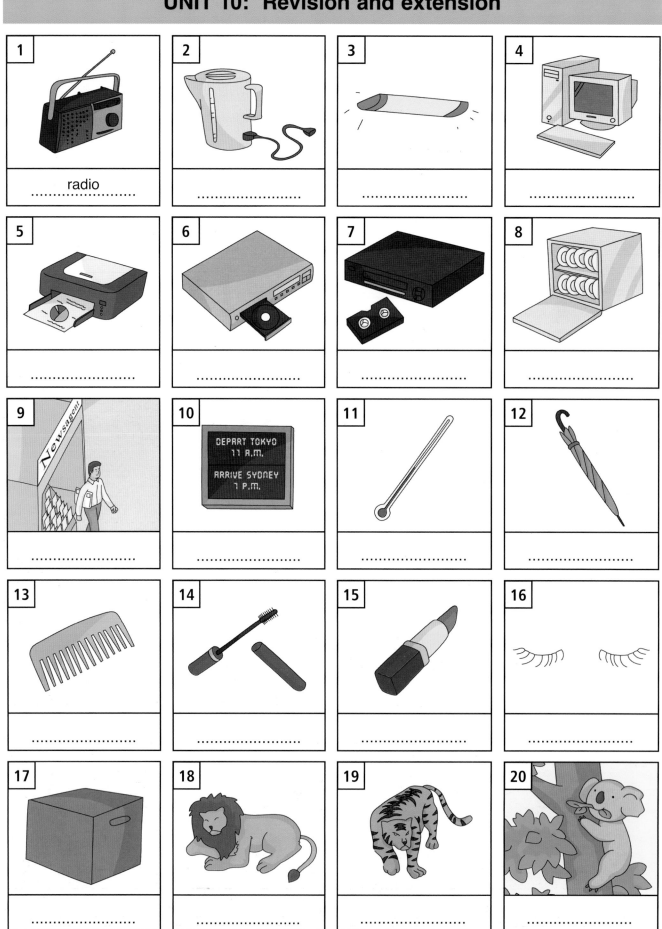

1. radio
2. ....
3. ....
4. ....
5. ....
6. ....
7. ....
8. ....
9. ....
10. ....
11. ....
12. ....
13. ....
14. ....
15. ....
16. ....
17. ....
18. ....
19. ....
20. ....

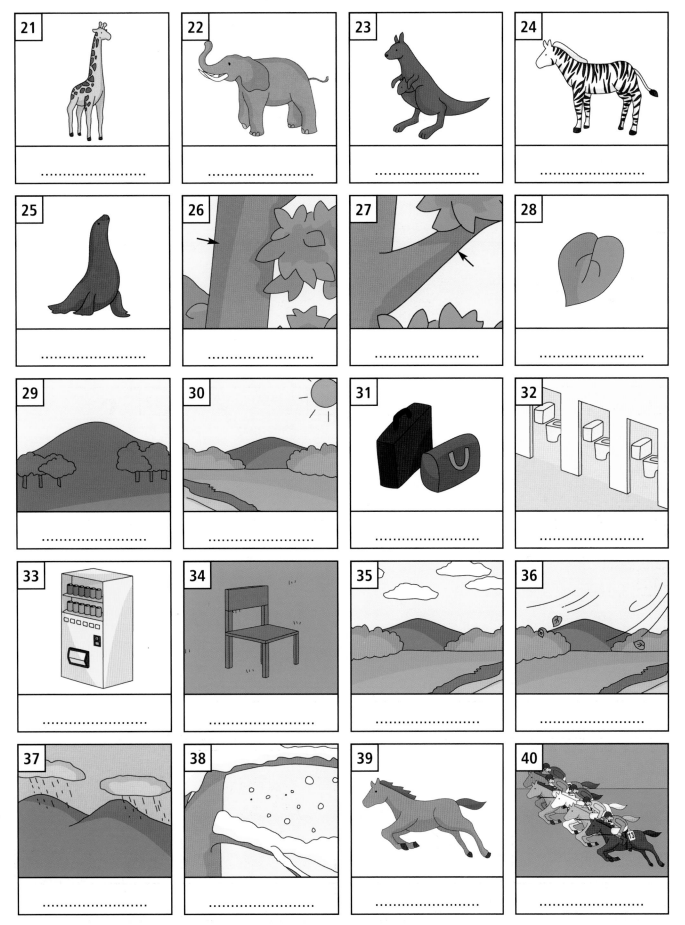

A

1. I'd rather watch TV than go swimming.
2. Can I help with the dishes?
3. Have you got your suitcase?
4. Are you ready to go?
5. Two to the airport, please.

a. Single or return?
b. Almost.
c. So would I.
d. Yes, I have.
e. No, it's all right.

B

1. Where's the camera?
2. I never watch TV.
3. Why did you buy a new house?
4. What time are we leaving?
5. Where are the toilets?

a. At a quarter past two.
b. I've got it.
c. Beside the entrance.
d. I didn't know that.
e. Because we needed more bedrooms.

C

1. Do you watch sport on TV?
2. When does the news start?
3. The radio's too loud.
4. Can you turn the TV off ?
5. Where are the tickets?

a. I'll turn it down.
b. I forgot them.
c. Six o'clock.
d. Sometimes.
e. Sure.

D

1. What channel's the movie on?
2. Can you turn the printer off?
3. We'd like to join a tour.
4. When does the tour finish?
5. Which video would you like?

a. At one thirty.
b. This one.
c. That'll be twelve dollars each.
d. Channel seven.
e. Where's the switch?

in   channel   open   about   where   beside   on

1 The tv and fridge are in here. You can get movies on channel 3.

OK, and where can I put my luggage?

2 Your suitcases can go .... the wardrobe. The bathroom is through there.

Good. What .... the phone?

3 The phone's .... that table. Ring nine for reception and three first for other calls.

Is there a fax?

4 Yes. It's .... there.

OK, and when does the restaurant .... for dinner?

5 At six o'clock.

Thank you.

Enjoy your stay.

without   might   rather   instead   down   enough   like   so

1
Can I help you?
Yes. I'd .... a large suitcase but it must be light.

2
Is that one big ....?
It's too big.

3
What about that one?
Yes. That looks OK. Could you get it .... for me?
Of course.

4
It's light enough, but I'd .... have one with wheels.
We .... have one. I'll check.

5
This one's for planes, ... it's very light and has wheels.
It looks OK.

6
It's light enough. How much is it?
$295.

7
Oh! How much was the one .... wheels?
$169

8
I'll take it ....

does	take	open	extra	start	from	tours	before

1
The Jameson Art Gallery. Colin speaking.

Good morning. When is the gallery ....?

2
The gallery's open .... nine a.m. to four thirty from Monday to Saturday. It's closed on Sundays.

Thanks. And how much .... it cost?

3
Seven dollars.

Do you have ....?

4
They're an .... three dollars.

When do they .... and how long do they take?

5
There are two tours. They .... two hours and start at nine thirty and one thirty. You need to arrive about fifteen minutes .... the start.

6
Thanks.

get   When   arriving   finish   Where   Why

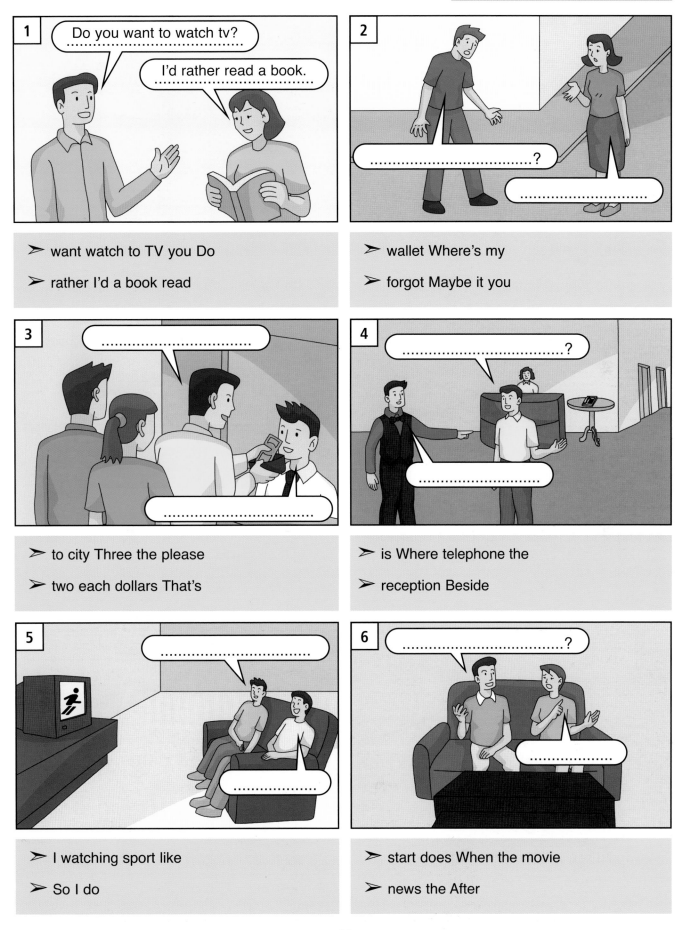

1

Do you want to watch tv?

I'd rather read a book.

➤ want watch to TV you Do

➤ rather I'd a book read

2

...........................?

....

➤ wallet Where's my

➤ forgot Maybe it you

3

....

....

➤ to city Three the please

➤ two each dollars That's

4

...........................?

....

➤ is Where telephone the

➤ reception Beside

5

....

....

➤ I watching sport like

➤ So I do

6

...........................?

....

➤ start does When the movie

➤ news the After

1
➤ late you Why are
➤ wrong went the restaurant I to

2
➤ buy suitcase we Can a new
➤ enough we got Have money

3
➤ taxi get Where I a can
➤ hotel the of front In

4
➤ a tour join like to I'd
➤ tour next starts The nine o'clock at

5
➤ would see you like movie Which to
➤ one This

6
➤ video do that Why you want
➤ It be might interesting.

Answers to Unit 10

Unit 10, page 86

1. radio	2. kettle	3. light	4. computer	5. printer
6. CD player	7. video	8. dishwasher	9. kiosk	10. timetable
11. thermometer	12. umbrella	13. comb	14. mascara	15. lipstick
16. eyelashes	17. box	18. lion	19. tiger	20. koala

Unit 10, page 87

21. giraffe	22. elephant	23. kangaroo	24. zebra	25. seal
26. trunk	27. branch	28. leaf	29. hill	30. sunny
31. luggage	32. toilets	33. vending machine	34. chair	35. cloudy
36. windy	37. rain	38. snow	39. horse	40. horse race

Unit 10, page 88

A. 1c 2e 3d 4b 5a   B. 1b 2d 3e 4a 5c   C. 1d 2c 3a 4e 5b   D. 1d 2e 3c 4a 5b

Unit 10, page 89

1. channel, where   2. beside, about   3. on   4. in, open

Unit 10, page 90

1. like   2. enough   3. down   4. rather, might   5. so   7. without   8 instead

Unit 10, page 91

1. open   2. from, does   3. tours   4. extra, start   5. take, before

Unit 10, page 92

1. Where   2. Why   3. get   4. When   5. finish   6. arriving

Unit 10, page 93

1. Do you want to watch TV?
   I'd rather read a book.

2. Where's my wallet?
   Maybe you forgot it.

3. Three to the city please.
   That's two dollars each.

4. Where is the telephone?
   Beside reception.

5. I like watching sport.
   So do I.

6. When does the movie start?
   After the news.

Unit 10, page 94

1. Why are you late?
   I went to the wrong restaurant.

2. Can we buy a new suitcase?
   Have we got enough money?

3. Where can I get a taxi?
   In front of the hotel.

4. I'd like to join a tour.
   The next tour starts at nine o'clock.

5. Which movie would you like to see?
   This one.

6. Why do you want that video?
   It might be interesting.

UNIT 11: I'm wearing one, too.

yourself

myself

herself

yourselves

themselves

ourselves

himself

wardrobe

dresser

chest of drawers

top drawer

bottom drawer

either

dress   wear

jeans   shirt

tie   socks

dress   skirt

tee shirt   jumper

jacket   coat

suit   hat

pants   bra

trousers   stockings

fall

clean

dirty

torn

burnt

hole

mark

creased

work

doesn't work

might be

must be

in case

worried

1

Come here Anna, and I'll dress you.

Where's Mom?

She's dressing Anna.

Anna, go and dress yourself.

1992

1996

2

Where's Anna?

She's in her bedroom. She's dressing herself.

Anna, where are you?

I'm in my bedroom. I'm dressing myself.

3

We're dressing ourselves.

They're dressing themselves.

96

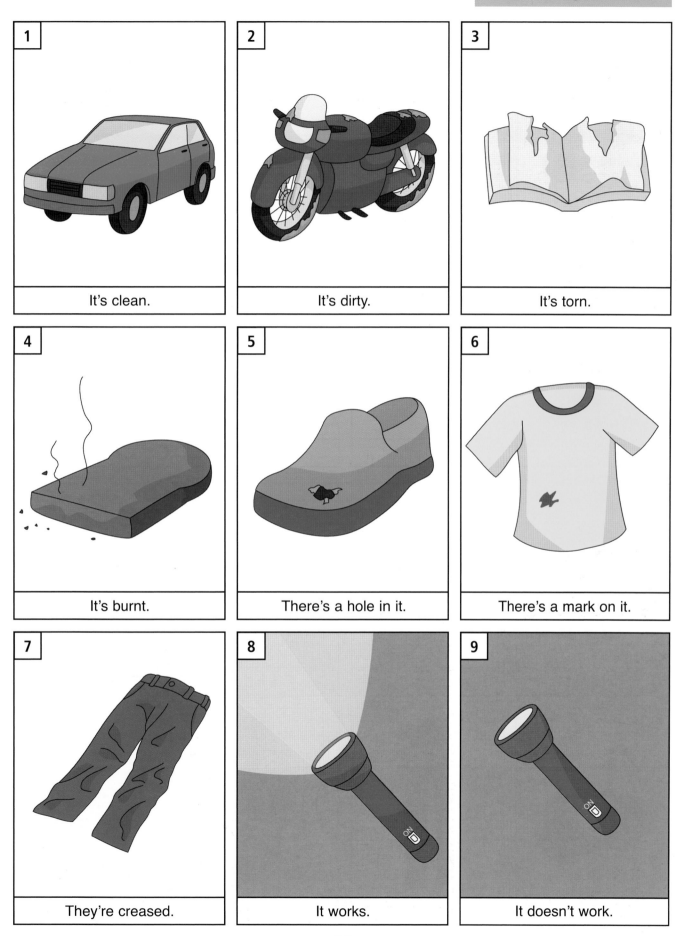

1. It's clean.
2. It's dirty.
3. It's torn.
4. It's burnt.
5. There's a hole in it.
6. There's a mark on it.
7. They're creased.
8. It works.
9. It doesn't work.

1 jeans	**2** a shirt	**3** a tie	**4** socks
5 a dress	**6** a skirt	**7** a tee shirt	**8** a jumper
9 a jacket	**10** a suit	**11** a hat	**12** a coat
13 a bra	**14** trousers	**15** stockings	**16** pants

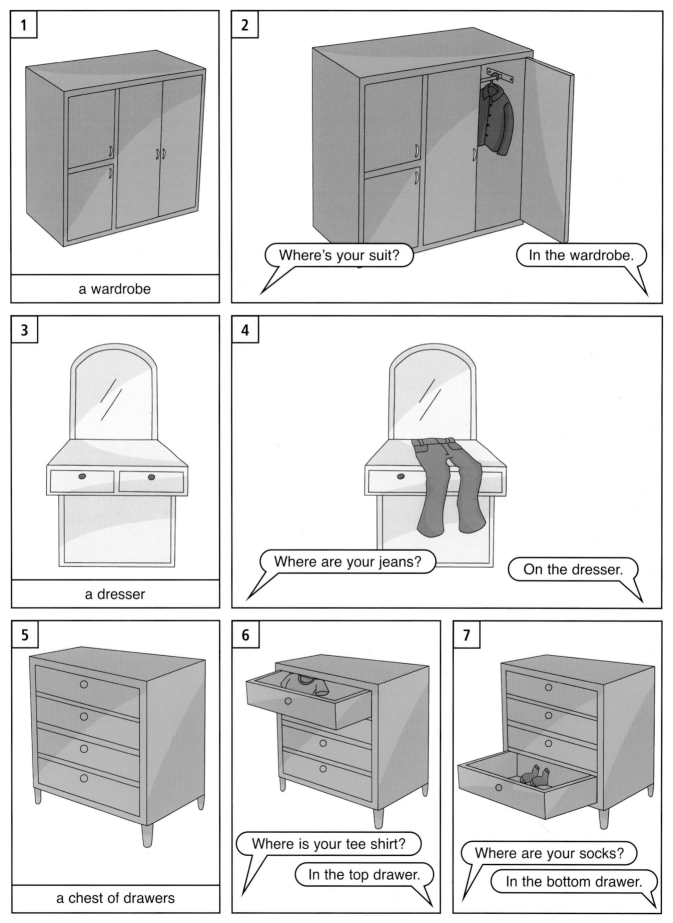

1 a wardrobe

2 Where's your suit? — In the wardrobe.

3 a dresser

4 Where are your jeans? — On the dresser.

5 a chest of drawers

6 Where is your tee shirt? — In the top drawer.

7 Where are your socks? — In the bottom drawer.

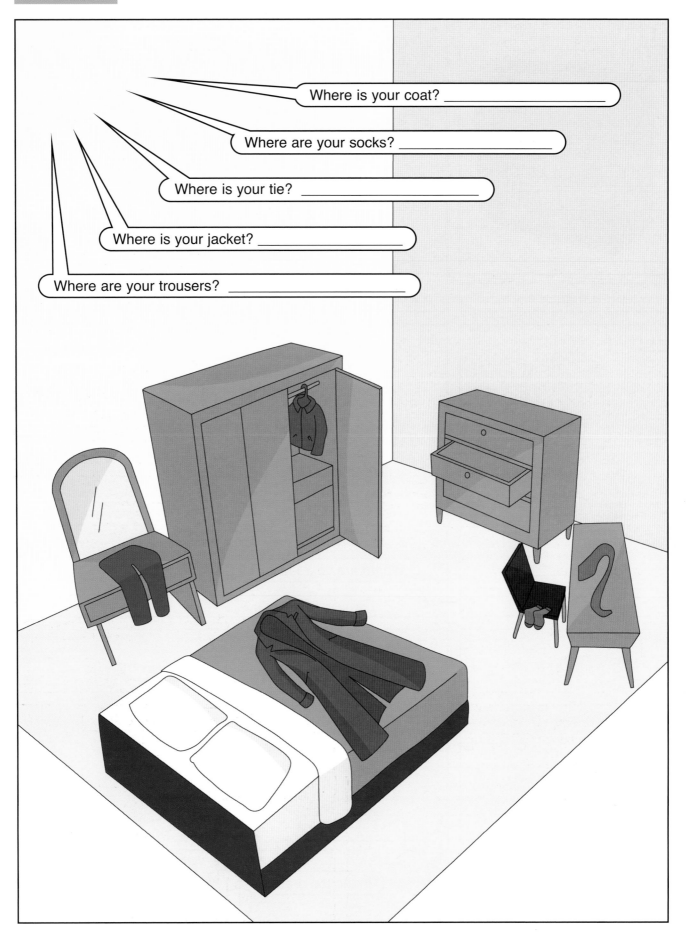

Where is your coat? _____

Where are your socks? _____

Where is your tie? _____

Where is your jacket? _____

Where are your trousers? _____

The Bensons

105

UNIT 12: You'd better go to the dentist.

you'd better
good idea

dentist
x-ray

motorbike
truck

happy
unhappy
comfortable
uncomfortable
done up
undone
safe
unsafe
pack
unpack

room

bench

hurry

have it ...ed

move
fix

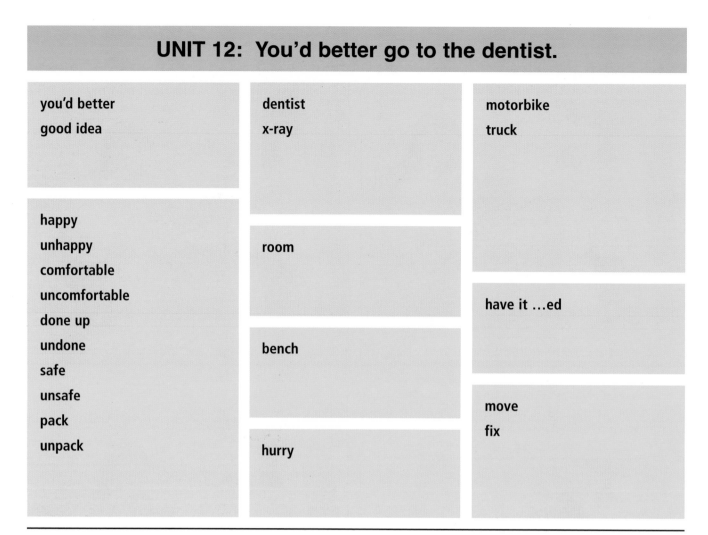

1 happy

2 unhappy

3 comfortable

4 uncomfortable

5 done up

6 undone

7 packed

8 unpacked

9 safe

10 unsafe

11

He's too big. There's not enough room for him.

Now there is enough room for me.

1	2	3
a sofa	a bench	A sofa is more comfortable than a bench.

4	5	6
a coat	a tee shirt	A coat is warmer than a tee shirt.

7	8	9
a truck	a motorbike	A truck is safer than a motorbike.

The Bensons

UNIT 13: I was having breakfast when the phone rang.

tongue
arm
finger
thumb
eye
nose
mouth
hair
knee
chest

take off
put on

until
soon

show

careful
careless
caution
danger

itchy
swollen
rash
bite
scratch
cough
bruised
cut

band aid
tablet
prescription
medicine
bandage
crutches
rest
stay in bed
stop smoking
exercise

birthday

few

1 I was having breakfast when the phone rang.

2 It was my mother. I was talking to her when the door-bell rang.

3 It was my father. I was talking to my father at the front door when the post-man came and gave me a letter.

4 It was from my brother. I was reading the letter from my brother when my mobile phone rang.

5 It was my sister.

6 They all said "Happy birthday!"

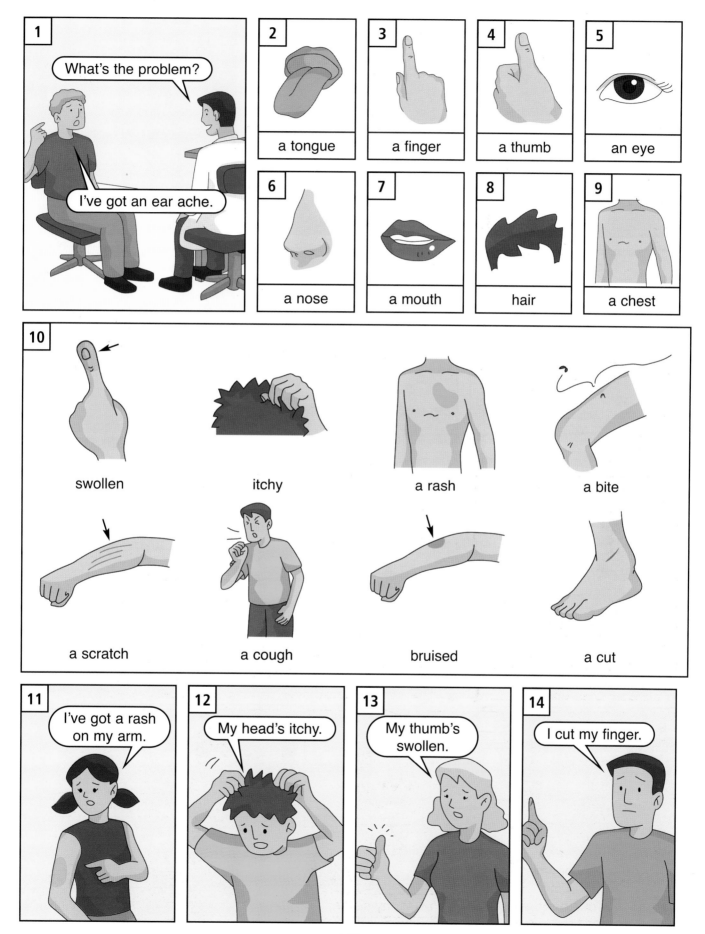

The Bensons

UNIT 14: Do you have a receipt?

borrow   lend

saw   drill
hammer   battery

handbag   scarf

plus   minus
multiplied by   divided by
equals   percent
point

limit
unlimited

I'm afraid

distance   length
width   height

high   wide
long   far

centimeter   kilometer
meter

for sale   rent
car rental firm

sign   signature
form   fill out a form

include

wheel
registration number
mirror
lights
damage
driver's license
panel beater

discount   exchange
refund   deposit
cheque   receipt

insurance (company)

windsurfer

a saw

Can I borrow your saw, please?

OK.

Thank you.

Alan was sawing some wood when his saw broke. He went next door to borrow Jeff's saw. Jeff agreed and gave Alan the saw. Alan finished sawing the wood and brought the saw back to Jeff.

1

$+$	$-$	$\times$	$\div$	$=$	$\%$	$\cdot$
plus	minus	multiplied by	divided by	equals	percent	point

2 Eight plus four equals twelve.

$$8 + 4 = 12$$

3 Eight minus four equals four.

$$8 - 4 = 4$$

4 Eight multiplied by four equals thirty-two.

$$8 \times 4 = 32$$

5 Eight divided by four equals two.

$$8 \div 4 = 2$$

6 Fifty percent of eight equals four.

$$50\% \text{ of } 8 = 4$$

7 Twenty five percent of ten equals two point five.

$$25\% \text{ of } 10 = 2.5$$

8

a battery

9

$8 includes batteries

Total price $8

10

$1 each

$7 batteries not included

Total price $9

11

I'll take these.

That's $100, please.

Does that include 10% discount?

No. I'm sorry. I forgot.

So it's $100 minus $10. The total price is $90.

Thank you.

10% Discount Today

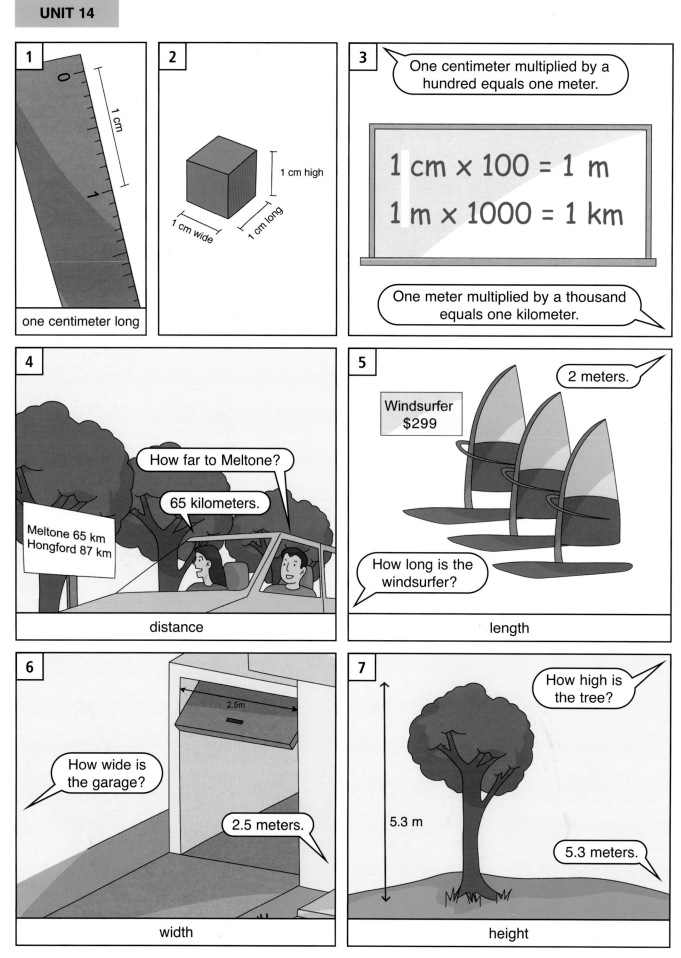

1. one centimeter long

2. 1 cm high / 1 cm wide / 1 cm long

3. One centimeter multiplied by a hundred equals one meter.

$$1\ cm \times 100 = 1\ m$$
$$1\ m \times 1000 = 1\ km$$

One meter multiplied by a thousand equals one kilometer.

4. How far to Meltone?

65 kilometers.

Meltone 65 km
Hongford 87 km

distance

5. Windsurfer $299

2 meters.

How long is the windsurfer?

length

6. How wide is the garage?

2.5m

2.5 meters.

width

7. How high is the tree?

5.3 m

5.3 meters.

height

The Bensons

1 wardrobe	**2**	**3**	**4**
5	**6**	**7**	**8**
9	**10**	**11**	**12**
13	**14**	**15**	**16**
17	**18**	**19**	**20**

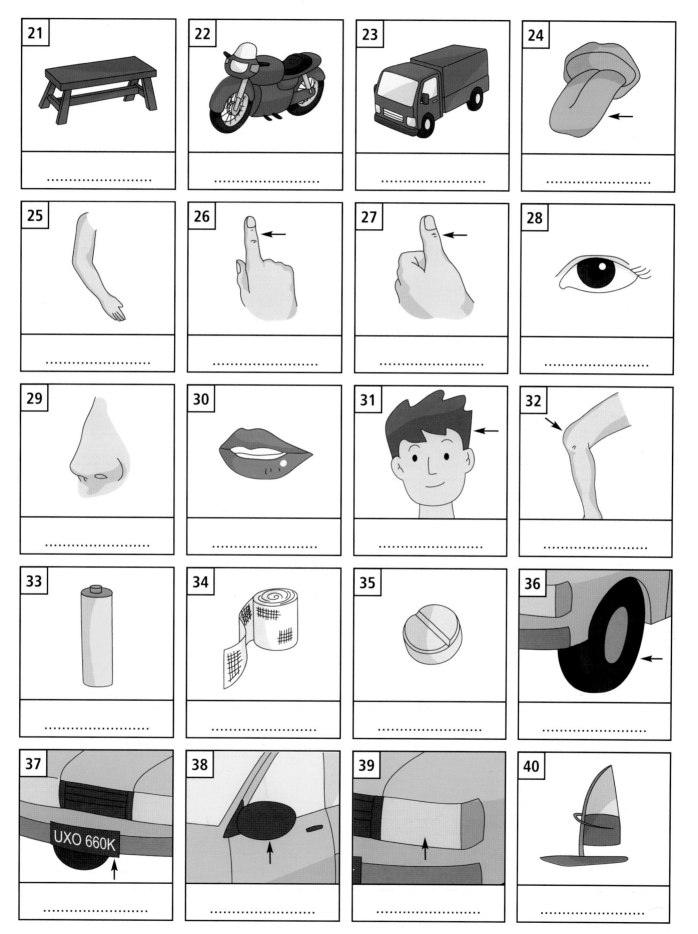

A

1. What's the matter?   a. You'd better have it fixed.

2. Does it hurt?   b. Good idea.

3. Where's my tee shirt?   c. Yes, it does.

4. We'd better go home.   d. In the top drawer.

5. My watch is broken.   e. I hurt myself.

B

1. What's the problem?   a. You should get a refund.

2. I've got a bad cough.   b. OK.

3. Will the bus come soon?   c. You should stop smoking.

4. There's a mark on my new shirt.   d. My finger's swollen.

5. Sign here please.   e. In a few minutes.

C

1. I've burnt my hand.   a. It might be in the car.

2. I'm very tired.   b. Yes, 10%.

3. I've got a toothache.   c. You might need a bandage.

4. Does that include a discount?   d. You'd better go to the dentist.

5. Where's the umbrella?   e. You need to rest.

D

1. My hand's swollen.   a. Sure.

2. I'm cold.   b. You'd better get another one.

3. Can I borrow your pen?   c. You'd better see a doctor.

4. This chair's uncomfortable.   d. Yes, 10%.

5. Do you need a deposit?   e. You should put on a jumper.

show   you   to   better   refund   on

too,   before   your   rather   deposit   one

1

This one looks good.

TO RENT

I'd .... have this one.

2

Can I help you?

We'd like to rent this one.

TO RENT

No, this one.

3

Have you been windsurfing ....?

TO RE No.

Yes, but not much.

4

Then that one's too long and much .... heavy. You should take the smaller .... but you'd better be careful.

OK. How much is it?

5

Twenty dollars per hour and a refundable .... of a hundred dollars.

OK.

6

And I'll need .... name, address and signature here.

TO RENT

Sure.

should   borrow   know

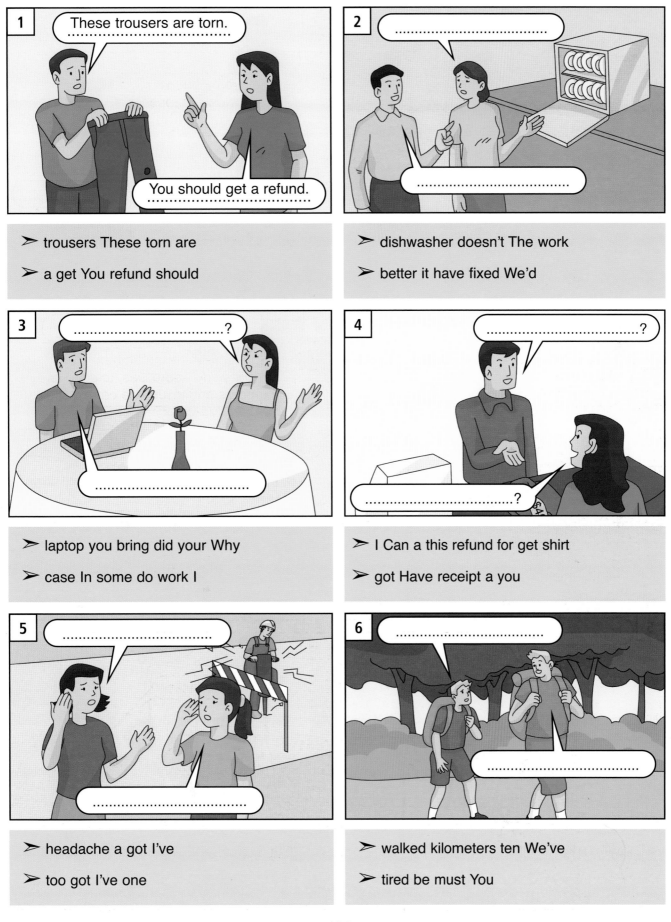

1

These trousers are torn.

You should get a refund.

➢ trousers These torn are

➢ a get You refund should

2

➢ dishwasher doesn't The work

➢ better it have fixed We'd

3

➢ laptop you bring did your Why

➢ case In some do work I

4

➢ I Can a this refund for get shirt

➢ got Have receipt a you

5

➢ headache a got I've

➢ too got I've one

6

➢ walked kilometers ten We've

➢ tired be must You

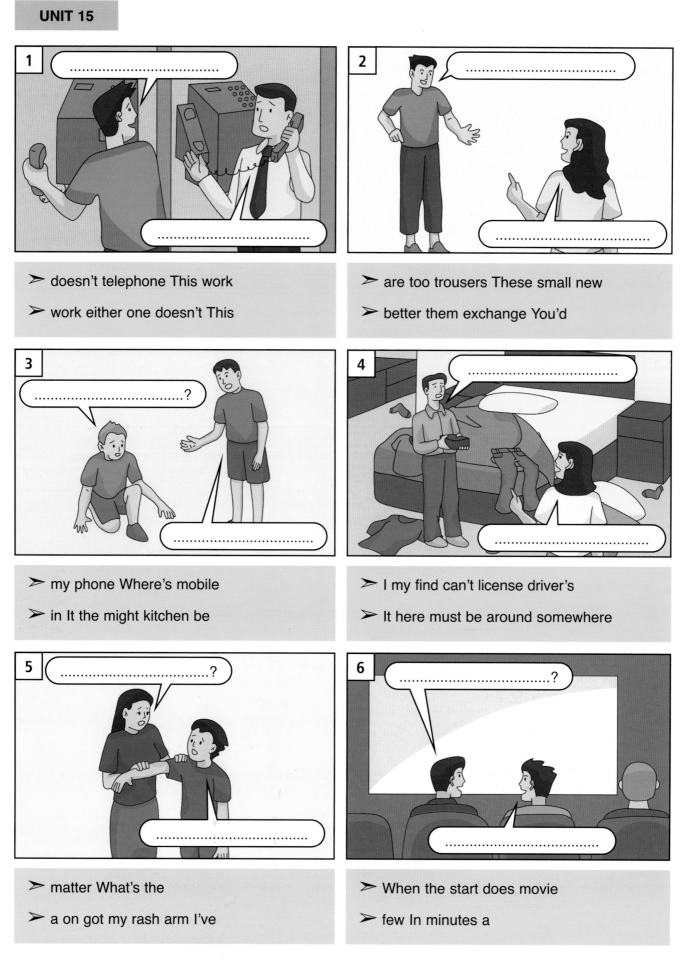

1
➤ doesn't telephone This work
➤ work either one doesn't This

2
➤ are too trousers These small new
➤ better them exchange You'd

3
➤ my phone Where's mobile
➤ in It the might kitchen be

4
➤ I my find can't license driver's
➤ It here must be around somewhere

5
➤ matter What's the
➤ a on got my rash arm I've

6
➤ When the start does movie
➤ few In minutes a

Answers to Unit 15

Unit 15, page 132

1. wardrobe
2. dresser
3. chest of drawers
4. top drawer
5. bottom drawer
6. shirt
7. jeans
8. tie
9. socks
10. dress
11. skirt
12. tee shirt
13. jumper
14. coat
15. suit
16. hat
17. pants
18. bra
19. trousers
20. stockings

Unit 15, page 133

21. bench
22. motorbike
23. truck
24. tongue
25. arm
26. finger
27. thumb
28. eye
29. nose
30. mouth
31. hair
32. knee
33. battery
34. bandage
35. tablet
36. wheel
37. registration number
38. mirror
39. lights
40. windsurfer

Unit 15, page 134

A. 1e 2c 3d 4b 5a   B. 1d 2c 3e 4a 5b   C. 1c 2e 3d 4b 5a   D. 1c 2e 3a 4b 5d

Unit 15, page 135

1. on, better   3. show   4. to, refund   5. you

Unit 15, page 136

1. rather   3. before   4. too, one   5. deposit   6. your

Unit 15, page 137

1. new   2. when   3. to   4. there's, the
5. doesn't   6. it, few   7. If   8. at

Unit 15, page 138

2. know   3. should   4. borrow

Unit 15, page 139

1. These trousers are torn.
   You should get a refund.

2. The dishwasher doesn't work.
   We'd better have it fixed.

3. Why did you bring your laptop?
   In case I do some work.

4. Can I get a refund for this shirt?
   Have you got a receipt?

5. I've got a headache.
   I've got one too.

6. We've walked ten kilometers.
   You must be tired.

Unit 15, page 140

1. This telephone doesn't work.
   This one doesn't work either.

2. These new trousers are too small.
   You'd better exchange them.

3. Where's my mobile phone?
   It might be in the kitchen.

4. I can't find my driver's license.
   It must be around here somewhere.

5. What's the matter?
   I've got a rash on my arm.

6. When does the movie start?
   In a few minutes.

price
half price
sale
special

anything else

try on
size
just right

over there

other
other one
same

pair of

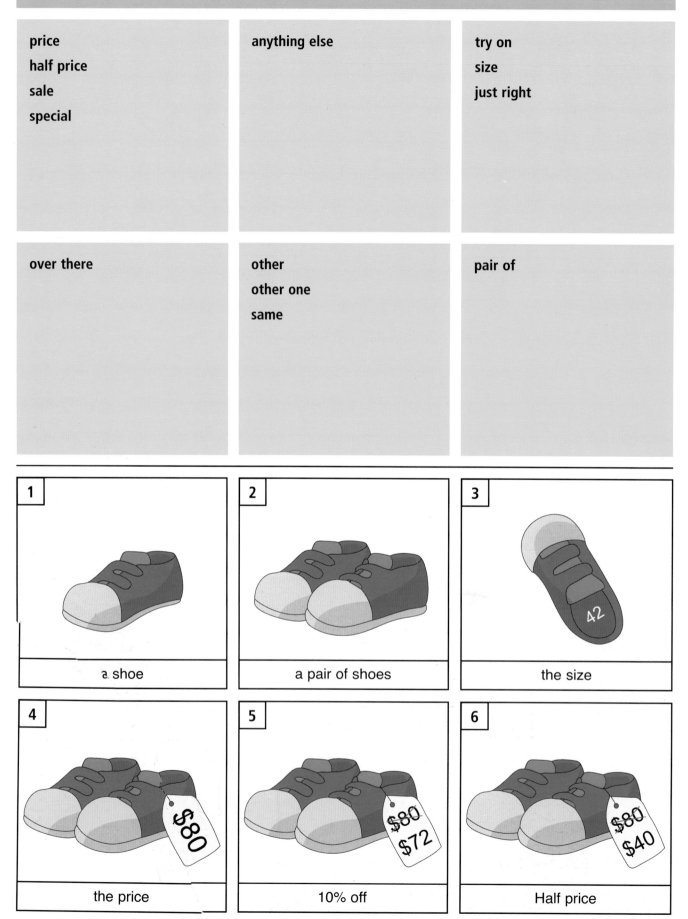

1 a shoe

2 a pair of shoes

3 the size

4 the price

5 10% off

6 Half price

1. I'll have a hamburger, thanks.

2. Would you like anything else?
   No thanks.
   That's $4.50, thanks.

3. I'll have a hamburger, thanks.

4. Would you like anything else?
   A bottle of water, thanks.

5. That's $6, thanks.

6. Which way to Macquarie?
   I'm sorry, I don't know
   Ask him.
   Which one? The one wearing a cap?
   No, the other one.

The Bensons

UNIT 17: Neither can I.

everywhere
everyone
everything

menu
entrée
main course
dessert
order
serve
service

recommend
delicious
terrible

onion
carrot
bean
peas
cabbage
cauliflower
tomato
potato
vegetable
bunch

plate
bowl
rice
soup

cow   sheep
pig   fish

beef
lamb
pork

until
so
neither

hungry
thirsty

swim

1 a cow — beef

2 a sheep — lamb

3 a pig — pork

4 a fish — fish

5 I'll have fish. So will I.

6

150

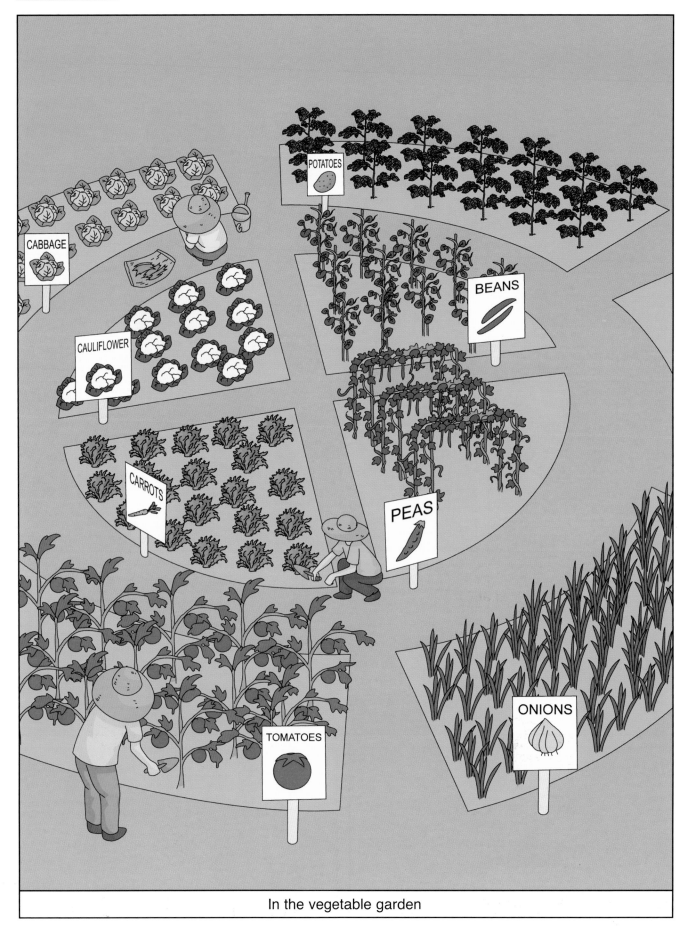

In the vegetable garden

The Bensons

158

UNIT 18: If I won, I'd buy a new car.

always
often
sometimes
rarely
never

as … as

empty
full

can't

a bowl	The bowl is empty.	The bowl is full.
a boy	I'm hungry.	I'm full.

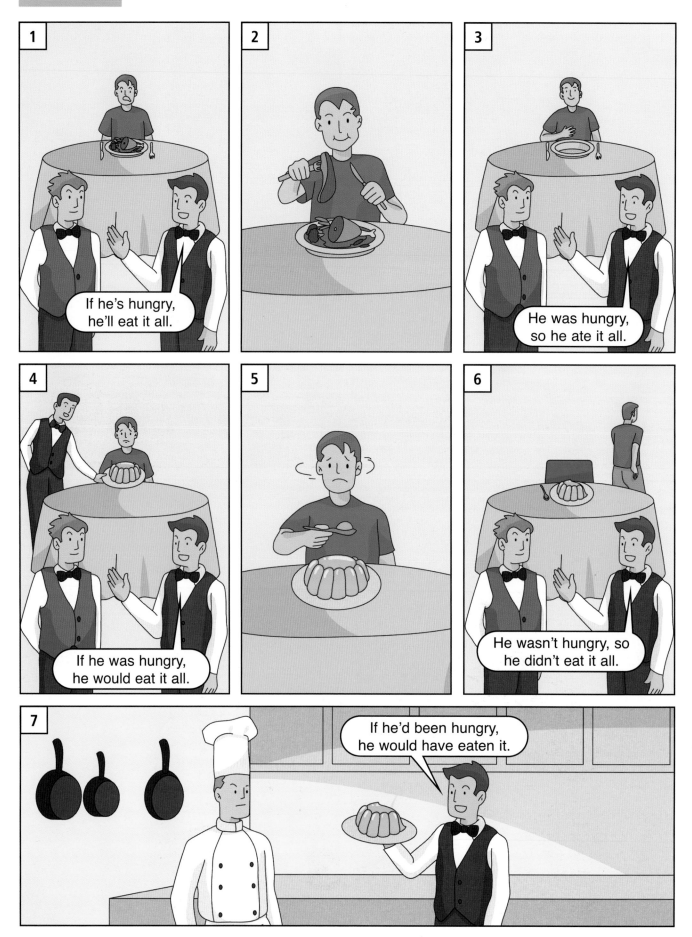

1 I always win.

If Paul wins again, he'll get another trophy.

2 I often win.

If Linda always won,
she'd have as many trophies as Paul.

3 I sometimes win.

If Tex won again, he'd get another trophy.

4 I rarely win.

If Louise won again, she'd be very happy.

5 I never win.

If Phil won a race, he'd get his first trophy.

6 I never won.

If George had won some races,
he'd have some trophies.

The Bensons

167

UNIT 19: I wish I could play the piano.

immediately
as soon as possible

congratulations
celebrate
well done

piano
violin
pianist
violinist

job advertisement
interview
apply
accept

good luck
bad luck
lottery

badly

change
go out

team

report

just a moment

wish

1
Rory saw an interesting job advertisement.

He applied for the job.

He went to the interview.

2 He got the job.

When can you start?

I can start next week.

He accepted the job.

I got the job.

He told his wife.

Congratulations. Well done!

He had a party to celebrate his new job.

1

before	change	after

2

before	change	after

3

I'd like to change my flight to the eleventh of October, please.

before	change	after

good luck

bad luck

a lottery ticket

I bought a lottery ticket.

Good luck.

Golden Lottery
Win $100,000
No. 845769

a team

My team lost.

Bad luck.

The Bensons

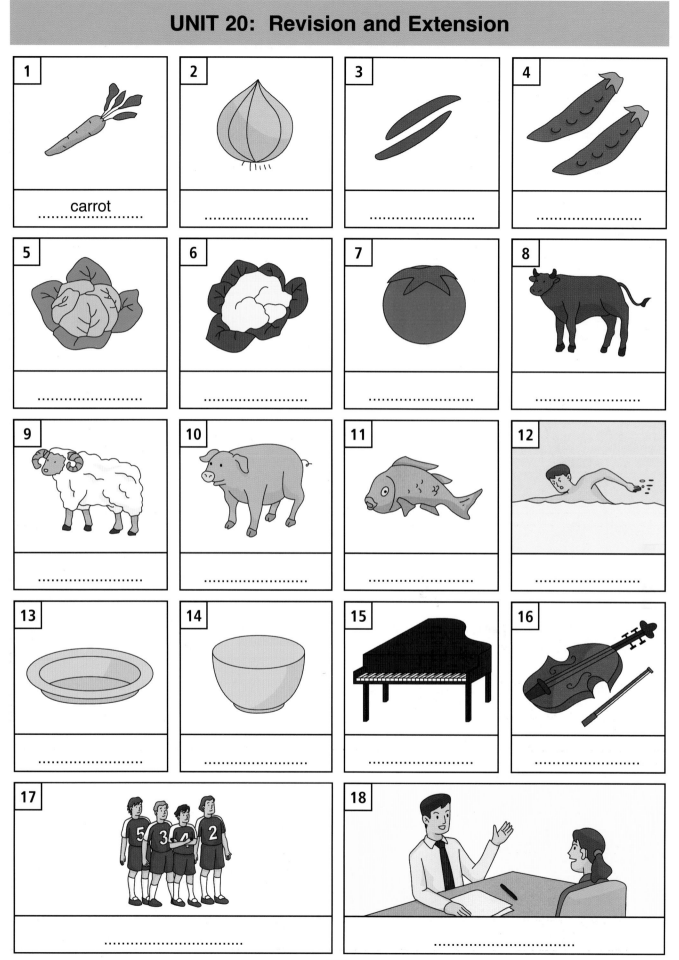

1 carrot

2 ....

3 ....

4 ....

5 ....

6 ....

7 ....

8 ....

9 ....

10 ....

11 ....

12 ....

13 ....

14 ....

15 ....

16 ....

17 ....

18 ....

A

1. Is your shirt too big?

2. I'll have a coffee, thanks.

3. Which way to the bank?

4. Your jeans look good.

a. That way.

b. Yes, but they're too short.

c. No, it's just right.

d. That's a dollar fifty.

B

1. He likes going to the movies.

2. I don't like cold weather.

3. They're not swimming today.

4. She can't speak French.

5. I'll have some fish.

6. I won't have an entrée.

a. So will I.

b. So does she.

c. Neither will I.

d. Neither can they.

e. Neither do I.

f. Neither are we.

C

1. I'm hungry.

2. I'm thirsty.

3. I'd like a hamburger.

4. I'd like some soup.

5. When should we leave?

a. I'd like some too.

b. As soon as possible.

c. You'd better eat something.

d. I'd like one too.

e. You'd better drink something.

D

1. When will you be back?

2. Can I try them on?

3. I've lost fifty dollars.

4. My job interview is this afternoon.

a. Bad luck.

b. Good luck.

c. Yes, of course.

d. In five minutes.

try   think   cost   take   too   reduction   would   for   better

was   So   full   I   enough   afraid   some   delicious   instead   have

1 Who'd like .... soup?

Yes, please.

2 Does it .... tomato in it?

Yes, it does.

I'm sorry. I'm ....
I don't eat tomato.

3 Oh. Would you like some bread and cheese .... ?

Yes, thanks.

4 Could I have some more soup? It's ....

Thank you.

5 Would you like some more bread and cheese?

No thanks. I'm ....
It was very nice.

6 Has everyone had ....

I'd like some more.

.... would I.

No thanks. I've had enough.

So have ....

7 That ....
lovely.

Yes, it was. Sorry about the tomato.

That's alright.

181

until   day   would   if   appointment   change   next

1

Amherst Medical Center. Can I help you?

Hello. This is Wendy Jones. I have an .... with Doctor Spelling this afternoon. I'm afraid I have to .... it.

2

OK. When would like to see him?

Well, Friday morning .... be good.

3

He's got appointments all .... on Friday. Would .... Monday afternoon be alright, after four o'clock?

Earlier would be better.

4

I'm afraid the doctor's busy .... four. The next appointment would be at nine on Tuesday morning.

I think that'll be OK. I'll have to check. Can I call you back?

5

That's fine. It would be good .... you could call back this morning.

Sure.

6

Thanks.

No problem.

before	again	everything	if	haven't	So	soon

1. It was lovely to meet you. We've really enjoyed it here.
.... have we. It's a pity you can't stay longer.

2. Yes. I hope we'll see you in New York.
Thanks. You've got our address .... you?
Yes, we have.

3. And .... you come to Sydney, you can stay with us.
That would be great.

4. We'll have to leave .... The taxi will be here in a few minutes.
OK. Are you sure we've packed .... ?

5. Yes. I checked .... we left the room.
We'd better go. The taxi's arrived.

6. Goodbye. Hope to see you .... soon.
Goodbye.

1
➤ shoes small these too Are

➤ right just they're No

2
➤ the long skirt too Is

➤ it's short too No

3
➤ big The jacket's too

➤ size I'll smaller get a

4
➤ is This small too

➤ larger a get I'll size

5
➤ coffee don't I want

➤ I Neither do

6
➤ long I talk can't

➤ can Neither I

1

➤ go to have I soon

➤ do we So

2

➤ go We movie that to won't

➤ we will Neither

3

➤ coke I'd a like

➤ too one like I'd

4

➤ time party is What the

➤ thirty Seven

5

➤ need you do a When flight

➤ possible soon As as

6

➤ back you When be will

➤ two hours In

Unit 20, page 178

1. carrot	2. onion	3. beans	4. peas	5. cabbage
6. cauliflower	7. tomato	8. cow	9. sheep	10. pig
11. fish	12. swim	13. plate	14. bowl	15. piano
16. violin	17. team	18. interview		

Unit 20, page 179

A. 1c 2d 3a 4b   B. 1b 2e 3f 4d 5a 6c   C. 1c 2e 3d 4a 5b   D. 1d 2c 3a 4b

Unit 20, page 180

1. better   2. try   3. think, too   4. for, cost   5. would   6. reduction   7. take

Unit 20, page 181

1. some   2. have, afraid   3. instead   4. delicious   5. full   6. enough, So, I   7. was

Unit 20, page 182

1. appointment, change   2. would   3. day, next   4. until   5. if

Unit 20, page 183

1. So   2. haven't   3. if   4. soon, everything   5. before   6. again

Unit 20, page 184

1. Are these shoes too small?
   No, they're just right.

2. Is the skirt too long?
   No, it's too short.

3. The jacket's too big.
   I'll get a smaller size.

4. This is too small.
   I'll get a larger size.

5. I don't want coffee.
   Neither do I.

6. I can't talk for long.
   Neither can I.

Unit 20, page 185

1. I have to go soon.
   So do we.

2. We won't go to that movie.
   Neither will we.

3. I'd like a coke.
   I'd like one too.

4. What time is the party?
   Seven thirty.

5. When do you need a flight?
   As soon as possible.

6. When will you be back?
   In two hours.

Answers to practice pages

Unit 1, page 7

1. father
2. daughter
3. brother
4. grandmother
5. sister-in-law
6. father
7. daughter-in-law
8. brother
9. daughter
10. cousin
11. uncle
12. aunt
13. sister
14. cousin
15. grandfather
16. nephew
17. niece
18. brother-in-law

Unit 7, page 66

4. Mom says <u>I can't go out</u>, because <u>it's raining</u>.

5. Mom says <u>I have to tidy my bedroom</u>, so <u>I can't go to the park</u>.

6. <u>We have to go now</u>, because <u>it's after ten o'clock</u>.

Unit 8, page 70

The flight <u>starts</u> at eleven o'clock and <u>finishes</u> at seven o'clock.

Unit 9, page 79

12. <u>Behind</u> the sofa.
13. <u>In front of</u> his house.
14. <u>Beside</u> the TV.
15. <u>Under</u> the bed.
16. <u>On</u> the table.

Unit 9, page 80

7. He <u>will</u> lift it.
8. He <u>won't</u> lift it.
9. He <u>might</u> lift it.

Unit 9, page 81

4. Yes.
5. No.
6. Maybe.

Unit 11, page 102

On the bed.   On the chair.   On the table.   In the wardrobe.   On the dresser.

Unit 14, page 123

4. Would you <u>lend me</u> your scarf, please?
5. I'd like to <u>borrow</u> $80,000, please.
8. He said he <u>doesn't have enough money to buy a car</u>, so <u>will have to rent one</u>.

Unit 16, page 146

4.1. I've got two cars.
4.2. One of them is new.
4.3. The other one is old.

Unit 19, page 172

1. I wish <u>I was rich</u>.
2. I wish <u>I had a big house</u>.
3. I wish <u>I played the violin well</u>.

Unit 19, page 177

12. <u>Goodbye</u>.

Grammar/Function/Topic in Volumes 1 and 2

Index for Volumes 1 and 2

189